11 Reasons Why You Will Never Sell Your Business For The Money You Deserve!

(And What To Do About It)

Justin K. Cauley

Justin K. Cauley

Copyright © 2011 Justin K. Cauley

Edited By Anabel Soto

Cover Design By George Suciu

Reviewed By A.P. Nadal

ISBN: 1461181526
ISBN-13: 978-1461181521

Profitmax Solutions
40 Wall St., 28th Floor
New York, NY 10005
www.profitmaxsolutions.com

Disclaimer

This book is designed to provide information in regard to the subject matter covered. It is sold with the understanding that the publisher, author, and advisers are not rendering legal, accounting or other professional services.

Every effort has been made to make this book as complete and as accurate as possible. However, there may be mistakes both typographical and in content. Therefore, this text should be used only as a general guide and not as the ultimate source of published information. Furthermore, this manual contains information only up to the printing date.

The authors, advisers and publisher shall have neither liability nor responsibility to any person or entity with respect to any loss or damage caused or alleged to be caused directly or indirectly by the information contained in this book.

This book is dedicated to business owners everywhere.

CONTENTS

Without one (a plan), you're better off heading down to the horse races and betting on the 'Win Three'.

Peter J. Patsula

INTRODUCTION

When owning a business it's important to understand how *"sellable"* your business is. This is often the biggest asset you own and your biggest source of income for retirement.

It has been reported that 75% or more of a business owner's net worth is tied DIRECTLY to the eventual sale of his/her business.

Unfortunately far too often we get caught up in the day to day operations that distract us from what I believe is the most important goal a business owner can have; that goal is creating and maintaining a business that is profitable and sellable, so you can sell on your terms for a fair price when you are ready.

Regrettably the truth is that roughly 80% of all small businesses are unsellable. Less than 85% of all small business owners have a plan in place to transfer ownership and only 5% of all small businesses that are up for sale get sold successfully.

With 75% or more of net worth being directly tied to the business itself, not being able to cash out when you're ready is simply not an option.

When that inevitable day comes (every owner will exit their business on their terms or otherwise) reality will strike and the overwhelming majority of business owners will be left with only two unacceptable options.

Unacceptable Option 1:

Sell what assets you have, if any. Your equipment and furniture will most likely get sold for a fraction of what they're worth.

Unacceptable Option 2:

Close your doors. Period.

You did not go into business to have either of those options become your ultimate fate.

Within these pages I've identified 11 reasons why the majority of business owners fail when it comes to exiting their businesses. I have also identified 10 commandments that will help you sell your business when you believe the time is right. **Be proactive!** Don't leave anything to chance. With enough time, planning and strategy, you can avoid being one of the over 3 million small business owners who cannot and will not sell their businesses successfully.

Become sellable,

Justin K. Cauley

"Turn your business into an asset someone will WANT to BUY."

Any fool can start a business. It takes a smart or lucky person to make it profitable. But it takes a genius to exit a business successfully.

Unknown

REASON #1:

YOU WILL BE OFF, WAY OFF

One of the most expensive mistakes a business owner can make is to not understand the approximate value of their business prior to entering the selling process. It is extremely important to know a ballpark value before making the decision to sell.

It is in every entrepreneurs best interest to work with somebody qualified to put a price on their business before the decision to sell is made. This will reduce the risk of you selling your business for less than it is worth.

More often than not there will be a price gap between what you think you can sell your business for and the estimated value created by a professional using the financial information you provide. The actual selling price of your business is ultimately determined by the market.

You can't sell your business for more than what someone else is willing to pay for it.

FYI: Businesses typically sell for, on average, 20% less than the listed price. If you have your heart set on a certain figure your business should be reasonably priced and valued higher. You should aim for a value at least 20% higher than your asking price.

*Ambition is a dream with a
V8 engine.*

Elvis Presley

It's not the plan that is important, it's the planning.

Dr. Graeme Edwards

REASON #2:

YOU WILL BE WOEFULLY UNPREPARED

Determining the initial price point of your business is only the first step. A business is undeniably not a house, but the same attention to detail before the sale is necessary. Financial and legal affairs should be current. Anything a potential buyer will want to see and should see must be recent, correct, and available for review.

Demonstrating readiness to sell your business places your company in a favorable light. In so doing, potential buyers will feel confident that everything is in order.

Most business owners underestimate the amount of paperwork and documentation that will be requested by potential buyers. Unless you are a master of record keeping you most likely won't have everything that will be requested. It can take weeks or months to put the kind of information together that will make your potential buyer feel comfortable enough to make a bid and eventually a purchase.

Get your financial house in order before you decide to exit. You don't want to lose momentum and you don't want to lose a deal because of a few missing pieces of paper.

If a man will begin with certainties he shall end in doubts; but if he will be content to begin with doubts he shall end in certainties.

Francis Bacon

Before everything else, getting ready is the secret of success.

Henry Ford

REASON #3:

YOU WILL TRY TO SELL YOUR BUSINESS WEARING **ROSE COLORED** GLASSES

Most business owners feel that their business is the best in the world however you have to place yourself in the position of the buyer. Ask yourself these important questions:

- Will your business put the new owner in a position to be successful?
- Will your business provide a good income stream for the new owner and their family?
- Would you want this business opportunity if you were looking to buy a business?

- Are you confident that the business can generate enough revenue to pay you if you decide to offer owner financing?

If you can honestly answer "Yes" to the above questions you should be in a very good position to exit your business successfully.

If you've answered "No" to any of the above questions then work on your business until you can objectively and honestly say "yes" and mean it.

I don't want yes-men around me. I want everyone to tell the truth, even if it costs them their jobs.

Samuel Goldwyn

The general who wins the battle makes many calculations in his temple before the battle is fought. The general who loses makes but few calculations beforehand.

Sun Tzu

REASON #4:

YOU WON'T HAVE A GOOD SELECTION PROCESS

The better you know the buyer, the easier it will be to sell your business. You have to approach the sale of your business realistically, understanding that a potential buyer will be doing the same.

By knowing the buyer, their motivations, their interests, their desires, and their background, you will be better equipped to make an informed decision about whether or not that buyer is the right person to operate your business.

You have to make sure the potential buyer is buying for the right reasons. "I've always wanted to have my own business" is not a good enough answer; remember a lot is at stake here.

I know of a business that went under after a sale because all key employees quit due to the new owner. The new owner turned out to be a bad fit for the business culture that had already been established.

In one case the seller wanted the buyer to take a personality test. That may sound crazy to you but the transition was very smooth and everyone was happy (especially the employees).

Any candidate interested in your business should be comfortable with business ownership and all that it entails. A potential buyer should also have a vision or a plan to improve and build upon what you have created without trying to kill what's working. Lastly, it is imperative that a potential buyer have a genuine interest and familiarity in the market or industry.

Depend on the rabbit's foot if you will, but remember it didn't work for the rabbit.

R. E. Shay

There is nothing more frightful than ignorance in action.

Goethe

REASON #5:

YOU WILL TRY TO COMPARE APPLES AND ORANGES

More often than not, this is what will happen during an initial negotiation: an offer will be presented and you will take one look at the price instantly declaring "NO!"; refusing to give the offer further consideration.

If you really want to sell your business successfully, you have to understand how a deal is structured in its entirety before you can give the thumbs up or the thumbs down to the arrangement. You can miss out on a great opportunity to cash out by weighing your decision too heavily on the initial price and offer.

Deciding to sell your business is an important step; make sure you understand every detail of the deal completely.

Don't be afraid to ask questions. For many business owners this will be the first and last time selling a business, ask as many questions as you need to ask in order to feel comfortable with the transaction.

The last thing you want to catch is a case of the *Should haves, Could haves, Would haves...*

It is better to know some of the questions than all of the answers.

James Thurber

We always plan too much and always think too little.

Joseph Schumper

REASON #6:

YOU WILL BE AFRAID TO "BREAK UP"

Successfully selling the business should always be the final goal when purchasing a business yet too many business owners lose sight of that. Business owners often become consumed with trying to construct the deal. It's because of this that owners fail to see a bad deal when it's staring them right in the face.

Investments of time, energy and money make it difficult for owners to end negotiations even when faced with an awful deal. In most cases however that is exactly what must be done. Do not be afraid to walk away from a bad deal.

In order for you to successfully sell your business everyone has to win, especially you! If the offer isn't right and cannot be fixed, there's no other choice but to walk away. It's far better to not execute a deal at all then to complete a bad deal. It will only hurt you and your bank account in the end.

Trust your gut and your advisory team. If your business is as strong as you think it is, selling it shouldn't be a problem. If you feel you're not absolutely *"winning"* in a transaction then pull the plug and wait for a more appealing offer.

Behold the turtle, he makes progress only when he sticks his neck out.

Bruce Levin

Trying to predict the future is like trying to drive down a country road at night with no lights while looking out the back window.

Peter Drucker

REASON #7:

YOU WILL HIT THE SNOOZE BUTTON ONE TOO MANY TIMES

Too many business owners wait until the very end to exit their business. You will wait until sales are down. You will wait until you are completely burned-out. You will wait until your business relationships are completely strained.

The period to sell your business is when business is good. The time to sell your business is before you're forced to do so.

Most entrepreneurs try to sell or exit their business in a down economy when prices are at their lowest rather than attempting to sell in a booming economy when prices are at their highest. This can cost you thousands of dollars.

The old proverb is that as an entrepreneur you should think about and plan to sell your business the day after the business is first purchased or created.

I know most business owners ignore that proverb when they begin their venture but once you commence thinking about exiting please take heed.

Remember reasons one through three?

Do not underestimate how long it will take to exit your business and more importantly do not overestimate how much your business is worth. Do not undervalue your business attractiveness to potential buyers.

Planning is an unnatural process; it is much more fun to do something. The nicest thing about not planning is that failure comes as a complete surprise, rather than being preceded by a period of worry and depression.

Sir John Harvey-Jones

All of us have bad luck and good luck. The man who persists through the bad luck - who keeps right on going - is the man who is there when the good luck comes - and is ready to receive it.

Robert Collier

REASON #8:

YOU WILL TRY TO SELL ICE TO AN ESKIMO

There are usually many more potential buyers than there are good businesses for sale. The million dollar question is how serious are those buyers?

90% of all buyers have never before owned a business. The majority of potential buyers start the process with serious intentions to make a purchase, but more often than not they end up backing out of the deal.

Some buyers will (unreasonably) want to close a deal if it is on their terms and conditions only. Other buyers will suffer from information overload leaving them incapable of making a decision. Finally you have the budding delusional entrepreneur who will focus solely on buying the "perfect" business which of course does not exist!

Most buyers only look with no real intention of ever making a purchase. You can't waste your time on those who aren't serious about purchasing your business. Many sellers will stop working with other potential buyers when one buyer shows interest, this can be a HUGE mistake.

Planning without action is futile, action without planning is fatal.

Unknown

A business plan is primarily an organizing tool used to simplify and clarify business goals and strategies, which might otherwise appear complex and intimidating.

Peter J. Patsula

REASON #9:

YOU WILL TRY TO FIT "I" INTO TEAM

How many NFL, NBA, MLB, NHL championships were won solely on the efforts of one person?

Selling a business will take a team effort. Unfortunately many business owners feel they and they alone are capable and responsible for making the sale because no one knows their business like they do. This may be true but selling a business successfully requires an entirely different set of skills—skills and resources that most business owners just don't have.

If you really want to win, you're going to need a complete team. Having a lawyer, accountant, business broker and a business advisor experienced in exit planning will greatly increase your chances of completing a successful exit. Not having a team around you can be a serious mistake.

How successful would Jordan have been without Pipen, Paxon, Armstrong, Kukoc and the rest of the team?

Teamwork is the ability to work together toward a common vision. The ability to direct individual accomplishments toward organizational objectives. It is the fuel that allows common people to attain uncommon results.

Andrew Carnegie

The way a team plays as a whole determines its success.

Babe Ruth

REASON #10:

YOU WILL SUFFER FROM THE "**HEFNER**" SYNDROME

Hugh Hefner once said that if he didn't have *Playboy*™ his life would come to an end. Most business owners experience an emotional upheaval during the selling process, especially during the final stages when they realize that a major chapter in their life will come to a close.

You may become conscious of the reality that when the business is sold, you will have nothing to do. This anxiety can cause your deal to fall apart. Subsequently you may decide that you just can't live without your business or you may fear your business can't survive without you—either way your transaction will be doomed.

It takes months and sometimes years to prepare mentally for life after a sale. If there is even an ounce of doubt in your mind about selling your business _don't begin the process_! Wait until your conscience is clear and you have a plan in place for your life *after* you exit.

Great is the art of beginning, but greater is the art of ending.

Henry Wadsworth Longfellow

Knowing is not enough, we must apply. Willing is not enough, we must do.

Goethe

REASON #11:

YOU WILL NOT HAVE AN EXIT PLAN

If you're looking to sell your business, working with a business consultant qualified in creating exit plans may be one of the best decisions you make.

A business consultant specializing in exit planning can give you the solutions needed to make your business more sellable. They can look at every aspect of your business and identify its strengths and its weaknesses in order to draw up a plan that is right for you and your business.

If you're faced with a valuation gap (the amount of money you need versus the actual value of the business as it stands today), retaining a business consultant to help conceptualize the solutions needed to increase revenue and profits will help make selling your business that much easier.

An exit plan is a great tool that can unquestionably increase the chances of you leaving your business on your terms when you are ready.

Having no plan is like sailing the seven seas without a compass, digging a ditch without a shovel, or hunting for pirate's treasure without an 'x' marks the spot.

Peter J. Patsula

The winners in life think constantly in terms of I can, I will, and I am. Losers, on the other hand, concentrate their waking thoughts on what they should have or would have done, or what they can't do.

Dennis Waitley

10 COMMANDMENTS TO A SUCCESSFUL EXIT

Now that we've talked about the reasons why the majority of business owners never sell or exit their business successfully, let's talk about what can be done to make sure it doesn't happen to you.

The first step in selling your business is feeling comfortable when saying "I am ready to start the process of selling my business." This could very well have been commandment #1, your success is directly linked to your mental readiness coupled with how well you have prepared your business for the sale.

Unfortunately, there's more to selling your business than just announcing a price and looking for a buyer.

The 10 commandments that I have identified are instrumental in successfully cashing out when you are ready to sell. I don't know of a single case where a business owner violated one of these commandments and was still able to exit their business without being hurt in the checkbook. The vast majority of business owners who never sell their business generally fail because of the 11 reasons previously mentioned and the violation of one or more of the commandments identified in the following chapters.

Even if you're on the right track, you'll get run over if you just sit there.

Will Rogers

Man is a goal seeking animal. His life only has meaning if he is reaching out and striving for his goals.

Aristotle

COMMANDMENT #1:

YOU MUST HAVE A REALLY GOOD REASON

Make sure you have a good reason for selling your business.

Please don't come to a decision to sell your business because you have had a bad week or because moving nearer to the grandkids sounds like a good idea.

Also, please don't choose to "test the waters" to see what kind of price your business will command. The first thing a prospective buyer will want to know is the reason you are selling.

A lame answer like "I'm really bored" simply won't do—well maybe for a knish stand but not a brick and mortar business. Be sure to have an authentic reason to answer the question. The more valid the reason you offer, the more serious the purchaser will be.

There are five main reasons why businesses get sold.

- The owner wants to retire.

- The owner dies.

- The owner has a serious health related issue (stroke, heart attack, cancer, etc.).

- The owner receives an unsolicited offer.

Make sure your reason for selling is genuine or your attempt to exit will be in vain.

Make your life a mission-not an intermission.

Arnold H. Glasgow

If you don't know where you're going, you'll end up somewhere else.

David Campbell

COMMANDMENT #2:

YOU MUST BE PREPARED

Don't wait until you have to sell for economic, emotional or personal reasons. Unfortunately unforeseen events such as illness or divorce happen.

The last thing you want is a low offer because of your circumstances. This happens when business owners are forced to accept low-ball offers because they're in a bind.

By keeping your business in sellable condition from inception you can still get top dollar for your company even in a distressed situation.

Creating and maintaining a living business plan in conjunction with an exit plan is a great way to sustain and increase the value of your business thereby insuring top dollar if ever you're put in an unexpected position of having to sell.

As they say, an ounce of prevention is worth a pound of the cure.

The secret to productive goal setting is in establishing clearly defined goals, writing them down and then focusing on them several times a day with words, pictures and emotions as if we've already achieved them.

Denis Waitle

All you have to do is know where you're going.

Earl Nightingale

COMMANDMENT #3:

YOU MUST HAVE YOUR DUCKS IN A ROW

Once you have made the decision to sell and *before* having a conversation with your business broker (I seriously advise you to retain one), you should gather the information needed to market and eventually sell your business.

Below is a list of some of the information you should collect and have prepared ahead of time.

- Profit and loss statements for the business for the previous three years

- Federal income tax returns for the business for the previous three years

- A list of fixtures and equipment

- The lease and any lease-related documents

- Copy of the franchise agreement (if applicable)

- List of loans against the business with amounts and payment schedule

- Copies of any equipment leases

- An approximate amount of the inventory on hand

- Names of outside advisors

The more information you have prepared ahead of time, the easier it will be in the long run.

Many people fail in life, not for lack of ability or brains or even courage but simply because they have never organized their energies around a goal.

Elbert Hubbard

Developing the plan is actually laying out the sequence of events that have to occur for you to achieve your goal.

George L. Morrisey

COMMANDMENT #4:

YOU MUST STAY ENGAGED

Remember you are part of the *I want to sell my business* team, your business broker can't do it all alone.

You may be asked on occasion to sit in on a meeting, open a little earlier or stay open a little later.

Your business broker will also advise you how and when to deal with possible buyers— there's a right time and a right way in which to engage them.

Your business broker may even ask you to work with an outside consultant when they feel it is in your best interest and if they feel it will help with the sale of your business.

Do what your business broker asks.

Follow your broker's advice and recommendations on the best way to bring about a successful sale.

<u>The more engaged you are in the process the better position you will be in to sell your business successfully!</u>

A goal is a dream with a deadline.

Napoleon Hill

All successful people have a goal. No one can get anywhere unless he knows where he wants to go and what he wants to be or do.

Norman Vincent Peale

COMMANDMENT #5:

YOU MUST REMEMBER LOOSE LIPS SINK SHIPS

Confidentiality works both ways.

As the seller, you must maintain confidentiality about a pending sale in your everyday business activities.

It will be extremely hard to sell your business if word gets out prematurely that you're in the process of exiting your company.

If you don't practice discretion, the relationships between you, your employees and your vendors may become strained which will definitely effect sales and morale.

Some of your key employees may even decide to leave. How attractive will your business become to a potential buyer if this happens?

Your loose lips could cause your business to become a sinking ship that no one wants to buy.

Remember to keep your impending sale confidential until the right time; you will be better off for it in the long run.

All who have accomplished great things have had a great aim, have fixed their gaze on a goal which was high, one which sometimes seemed impossible.

Orison Swett Marden

Let me tell you the secret that has led me to my goal: my strength lies solely in my tenacity.

Louis Pasteur

COMMANDMENT #6:

YOU MUST WALK A MILE

It is really important that you as the seller put yourself in the position of a potential buyer. The next time you go to your place of business, pretend you are a customer experiencing your company for the first time.

<u>It is important that potential buyers see your business at its best; busy, with no evidence of neglect</u>.

You should, at a minimum:

Keep normal operating hours. There is a tendency for sellers to "slack off" when they put their business up for sale.

Repair signs, replace outside lights, and do a general cleaning-up for the sake of first impressions.

Spruce up the interior and tidy the outside premises (if appropriate).

Repair or remove non-operating equipment.

Eliminate items that would not be included in the sale.

Maintain inventory at constant levels.

Provide great customer service.

Have friends or family members secret shop your business to make sure it's running at acceptable levels.

Business purpose and business mission are so rarely given adequate thought is perhaps the most important cause of business frustration and failure.

Peter F. Drucker

A person who aims at nothing is sure to hit it.

Unknown

COMMANDMENT #7:

YOU MUST SURROUND YOURSELF WITH THE RIGHT PROFESSIONALS

Only do business with professionals who understand the sales process.

For most business owners this will be the only time they sell a business and as a result this will be the biggest transaction (aside from real estate) that they will be involved in. Do not risk a successful sale by using a green or inexperienced business broker, lawyer or accountant.

I understand the role of nepotism, and I'm sure your golfing buddy is a great person but too much is at stake here to hire your friends daughter/son/niece/nephew, if they are not qualified or lack the skills.

Work only with seasoned professionals who know the business sale process. Inexperience can cost you a lot of money.

Remember roughly 5% of all businesses up for sale actually sell. Give yourself every advantage to having your transaction completed successfully.

Four steps to achievement: Plan purposefully. Prepare prayerfully. Proceed positively. Pursue persistently.

William A. Ward

I quickly learned that if I kept at it and plowed right through the rejections I would eventually get somebody to buy my wares.

Charles R. Schwab

COMMANDMENT #8:

YOU MUST BE FLEXIBLE

Make sure you keep the ball moving once an offer has been presented.

Just because you didn't get your requested price (that rarely happens), doesn't mean the offer was a bad one.

Study the offer closely and ask questions; ask a million questions if you have to. Make sure you understand the deal in its entirety before making a decision. The proposal presented may have some really good points that can compensate for the offering price.

Bigger payments, higher interest, a consulting agreement, more cash upfront than requested and the relationship between you and the potential buyer are examples of negotiation points that should be taken into consideration.

Most business owners spend years building and growing their business. In order to assure your business will continue to be successful, make sure the deal is a true win-win.

Don't be afraid to negotiate and do what you have to do to complete the deal.

As the old saying goes, the first offer presented will probably be the best offer you will ever get—this saying tends to almost always be true.

*There are only two options
regarding commitment.
You're either in or out.
There's no such thing as a
life in-between.*

Pat Riley

Without purpose ... goals, ambitions, and dreams aren't worth the paper they're written on. Without direction, a business plan, no matter how carefully written, is simply a bunch of words ruining a perfectly good blank sheet of paper.

Peter J. Patsula

COMMANDMENT #9:

YOU MUST REMEMBER THE GOLDEN RULE

Remember that most successful transactions are successful because they create a win-win scenario for everyone involved.

You will not prosper in the sale of your business if you think only of what's in it for you.

Keep in mind that your potential buyer is in the process of giving you a large sum of money, which they in all likelihood worked very hard to earn. They too have to feel comfortable and feel as if they are winning in the deal.

If you are sincere in wanting the buyer to win in the transaction as much as you yourself want to win then you should be in a great position to close your deal successfully. A transaction that is closed successfully is a transaction that both parties can walk away from happy.

All parties "winning" is exactly what has to occur if you want to successfully leave your business. Both parties have to feel as if they have received something of value. Both seller and buyer should feel as if they've won.

*Decide what you want,
decide what you are willing
to exchange for it. Establish
your priorities and go to
work.*

H. L. Hunt

The best way to predict the future is to create it.

Unknown

COMMANDMENT #10:

YOU MUST START EARLY

Make sure you give yourself and your business the opportunity to a successful sale by effectively planning for it.

Twelve to sixty months prior to wanting to sell is the ideal time to get started. The further in advance you plan the better. This will allow the time needed to get your business running as efficiently as possible; it will also provide a window in which to maximize value.

Do not leave money on the table by failing to do as much as you can to get the most out of your business.

If planning 12–60 months in advance could add thousands or even hundreds of thousands of dollars to your bottom line would you rush the process?

According to Mass Mutual, 75% of business owners that successfully sold their business reported to have wished they had begun the process sooner.

The difference between perseverance and obstinacy is that one often comes from a strong will, and the other from a strong won't.

Henry Ward Beecher

Perseverance is not a long race; it is many short races one after another.

Walter Elliott

HOW SELLABLE IS YOUR BUSINESS?

Getting yourself and your business in sellable condition will take quite a bit of work and a lot of preparation on your part. You know your business better than anyone, but do you know how to get it ready and in its best shape to sell?

Statistics show that selling your business successfully (creating the win-win and putting the most money in your pocket) is an extremely hard task to achieve.

More often than not, you will spend more time and money trying to sell only to take less than your business is worth. This often happens when sellers forgo the professional assistance needed to insure they receive the best price possible. In short, you will be leaving money on the table!

It is unwise to even think about selling your business without making sure you have done everything in your power to guarantee your business is in the best condition for a successful sale.

A powerful but obscure statistic in the business world is that roughly 80% of all small businesses up for sale never get sold (some business brokers suggest percentages as high as 90%).

Why does this happen? The businesses are unsellable!

It's because of this fact that I've developed the *P4 Business Enhancement & Value Maximization System*™. It's an extremely simple but powerful process designed to dramatically improve the appeal of one's business by increasing revenue, profit, cash flow and the salability factor.

By focusing on these 4 areas it's not only possible to increase the VALUE of your business by 50-100% or more, it is also possible to exponentially improve your odds of cashing out on your terms. This system was designed to be used for businesses of all sizes and can be applied to any industry.

The P4 System was designed to prevent your business from becoming another casualty among other small businesses.

Don't you want to be a part of the 5% club?

(Read on to find out what that is.)

In the next section I've described the *P4 Business Enhancement & Value Maximization System*™, provided a quick "salability" quiz and included a few case studies that show how the P4 Business Enhancement & Value Maximization System was implemented to help business owners just like yourself.

THE P4™ BUSINESS ENHANCEMENT & VALUE MAXIMIZATION SYSTEM

...a plan not only acts as your road map for success (a metaphor that's been beaten to death), it is your vehicle for prosperity...

Peter J. Patsula

STEP 1: (P1) PERFORM THE ANALYSES

WHAT PRICE CAN YOU SELL YOUR BUSINESS FOR NOW?

The valuation of your business is one of the most crucial steps and should not be taken lightly. Assessing the value of the business involves recasting profit-and-loss statements, owner's salary, perks and nonrecurring expenses.

We can help you find the initial value as well as create a plan to maximize that value in order to sell your business when you're ready for the highest price possible.

It is extremely rare for a business owner to be happy with the current value of their business. It is not uncommon to a see a valuation gap of 30-50%. That means if you believe your business is worth $500,000 your business will most likely be valued closer to $250,000 – $350,000 once a valuation has been completed.

If you take into account that most businesses on average sell for 20% less than asking price then you can assume you're at least 20% off of where your business's value should be—assuming you're happy with what that value is.

Always bear in mind that your own resolution to succeed is more important than any other one thing.

Abraham Lincoln

Chance favors only the prepared mind.

Louis Pasteur

STEP 2: (P2) PLAN FOR ACTION

WHAT PRICE DO YOU WANT TO SELL YOUR BUSINESS FOR?

Once the initial valuation is complete, we'll create a plan that will help you get the money you deserve by enhancing the salability of your business.

In this step we thoroughly go over all details of assessment (business valuation), craft the strategy to expand on what's working well, and address the weaknesses that can potentially rob value from your business.

There are certain "value drivers" that every business should have in place. Revenues are not the only thing that create a sellable company; in fact I wouldn't even name it as the number one driver of a business's value.

There are at least 10-20 different categories that help create the value and transferability of a business. You have to look at the whole picture if you ever want to exit your business successfully for the highest price possible.

Luck is a dividend of sweat. The more you sweat, the luckier you get.

Ray Kroc, Founder of MacDonald's

Let us not be content to wait and see what will happen, but give us the determination to make the right things happen.

Peter Marshall

STEP 3: (P3) PERFORM ENHANCEMENTS

GO FROM WHERE YOU ARE NOW TO WHERE YOU WANT TO BE

It is in this phase that your plan will take effect. Implementing your enhancement strategy will help you avoid leaving dollars on the table when it comes time to transfer ownership. You as a business owner need to ensure your business operates at full throttle completely independent of you.

Remember: the buyer is purchasing your business and not you. In order to successfully exit your business you cannot be a factor in the business's sustainability and growth.

With approximately 90% of all business buyers being complete "newbies" to business ownership (having never owned a business before) getting as close as possible to a turnkey operation is imperative.

No one wants to buy a job. Having your operation running profitably without you will be very appealing to a potential buyer.

Creating and maintaining a living business plan in combination with an exit plan is a great way to sustain and increase the value of your business thereby insuring top dollar if ever you're put in an unexpected position of having to sell.

This is the stage where the value gap in your business begins to close, creating a company that can realistically sell for your target value.

*Keep thy shop and thy shop
will keep thee.*

B. Franklin

A great fortune depends on luck, a small one on diligence.

Chinese Proverb

STEP 4: (P4) PREPARE FOR EXIT

NOW IS THE TIME TO SELL YOUR BUSINESS

The type of exit plan is dependent on the type of sale being conducted and how involved you as the business owner will be after the sale has been concluded. Most importantly you the business owner must be protected when you finally sell your business—both financially and legally.

We can't count the number of sales that fall through at the last minute. Completing the sale of a business is as much an art as it is a science. With our guidance you will not only have technique on your side but also an eye for excellence.

There are at least 80 pieces of documentation that need to be presented to a buyer not to mention issues that have to be resolved with your employees, vendors, and customers.

In this stage we gather and organize the book of information that will be presented to potential buyers as well as formulate strategies to handle any employee, vendor, and customer issues

With this information the business broker you choose will have a much easier time marketing your business once the due diligence phase begins. Having your book of documentation prepared and complete will only enhance your business desirability.

The due diligence phase is often the phase that can kill your deal. You must get a handle on all your documents as soon as possible.

THE "*LUCKY*" 5%

If you followed 100 entrepreneurs on their journey of business ownership what you would find is that after 5 years of tenure 50 would still be in business.

After 10 years in business, that number gets reduced even further. Only 30 entrepreneurs would still have "keys to the store."

Now if those 30 veteran business owners decided it was time to cash out only 5 would achieve their goal.

In other words you have only a 5% chance of selling your business after putting in 10 years of blood, sweat, and tears. If you said "I'll just exit after 5 years", then congratulations, your odds improved to a **whopping 8%.**

What side of the equation do you want to be on?

Get your business in shape today even if you feel you're 10 years away from considering cashing out.

No excuses.

You're invited to take our FREE Peak Performance and Salability Assessment to get a better understanding of the attractiveness of your business.

PLEASE SEND YOUR REQUEST TO
INFO@PROFITMAXSOLUTIONS.COM
OR LOG ON TO
WWW.PROFITMAXSOLUTIONS.COM

Some people dream of success... while others wake up and work hard at it.

Unknown

Diligence is the mother of good luck.

B. Franklin

TAKE THE SALABILITY QUIZ!

If you can answer yes to all the questions below you should be in a good position to exit your business on your terms when you're ready.

If you answer no to any of the below questions, you may want to focus on that area sooner rather than later.

1. Do you have at least 10 marketing strategies active at all times?

2. Do you measure all of the variables of your sales process, including such things as average number of appointments before the sale, the conversion rate (prospect to client), sales cycle, etc.?

3. Do you survey customers regularly to see how you are performing?

4. Do you have an effective and formalized hiring and training system?

5. If you were absent from the business for six months, would your business continue to grow?

6. Do you review your financial statements at least on a monthly basis?

7. Do you use Key Performance Indicators to measure the effectiveness of marketing, sales, customer service, and other areas of the business?

8. Do you spend most of your time working ON your business (planning, etc.) rather than IN your business (everyday tasks)?

How did you do on the quiz?

If you would like a more detailed evaluation of your business you are invited to take our FREE Peak Performance and Salability Assessment to better understand the attractiveness of your business.

PLEASE SEND YOUR REQUEST TO
INFO@PROFITMAXSOLUTIONS.COM
OR LOG ON TO
WWW.PROFITMAXSOLUTIONS.COM

It's the constant and determined effort that breaks down all resistance and sweeps away all obstacles.

Claude M. Bristol

CASE STUDIES

CASE STUDY 1

Technology Company Looking to Sell to a Third Party

Overview

The owner of a technology company needed to sell due to health issues. The owner was seeking $2 million; after 11 months there were over ten interested parties but no offers.

Major Issues

There was a big price gap between what the owner wanted and needed and the current estimated fair market value.

90% of the revenue the business generated was specifically tied to the owner's efforts.

Results

After implementing the P4 System the owner's contribution to revenue generation was reduced by 30% to date with a target of 0% responsibility of revenue generation. The business was relisted after 6 months completely turnkey for the new business owner. The anticipated selling price will meet both current market conditions and owner's needs.

"You seriously saved me; I thought I was going to have to liquidate everything, leaving me with virtually nothing. Your system made an almost impossible situation bearable. Thanks." R.N.

To accomplish great things, we must not only act but also dream, not only plan but also believe.

Anatole France

Wisdom is knowing what to do next, skill is knowing how to do it, and virtue is doing it.

David Starr Jordan

CASE STUDY 2

Limo Company Transferring Ownership to Next Generation

Overview

The owner of a 15 year old limo company wanted to transfer the business to his son. Even though the business was profitable and growing, the owner knew that his son was not in a position financially to buy the business.

Major Issues

The business was not positioned to provide a cash buyout to the owner.

The son did not have the capital necessary to buyout the father completely.

Results

A comprehensive plan was put in place that addressed the two major issues stated above. The owner's exit window was moved out 36 months, providing enough time to accomplish the family's objectives.

"I'm really glad I contacted you when I did. If I had tried to transfer my business without knowing this information we would have been in big trouble. Now we have a plan in place that will satisfy both of our needs without straining the business". J.W. & S.W.

Achievement results from work realizing ambition.

Adam Ant

Nothing is more terrible than activity without insight.

Thomas Carlyle

CASE STUDY 3

Commercial Cleaning Company Looking for Partnership Buyout

Overview

The founder of a commercial cleaning company wanted to buyout his partner and retain 100% ownership. A deterioration in their relationship was causing profitability and morale to become severely compromised, putting the entire business in jeopardy.

Major Issues

Disagreement on business value.

Business was not profitable enough to finance partnership buyout.

Results

Using the P4 Business Enhancement and Value Maximization System and taking into consideration the partner's goals, a plan was put in place to get the business back on track to profitability and provide a fair value for the buyout. Both parties wanted the business to provide as much of the financing as possible.

"We haven't seen eye to eye for years on a lot of issues, but retaining you and implementing the P4 system was one of the smartest decisions we've made in a long time". F.K.

I found every single successful person I've ever spoken to had a turning point. The turning point was when they made a clear, specific unequivocal decision that they were going to achieve success. Some people make that decision at 15 and some people make it at 50, and most people never make it at all.

Brian Tracey

Drive your business! Let not that drive thee.

Benjamin Franklin

IMPORTANT FACTS TO REMEMBER

90% or more of business owners will not be able to sell their business and meet their retirement cash requirements. *(Deliotte & Touche)*

80% of all small businesses are unsellable. *(Business Broker Press)*

85% or more of business owners do not have a plan in place to transfer ownership. *(Leading CPA Firm)*

75% or more of business owners net worth is tied directly to the sale of their business. *(Leading CPA Firm)*

75% of business owners surveyed who sold their business successfully wished they'd started the process sooner. *(Mass Mutual)*

Justin K. Cauley

71% of all small and medium sized business owners plan to exit their business within the next 10 years. *(Deliotte & Touche)*

65% or more of entrepreneurs do not know the value of their company. *(Leading CPA Firm)*

You're invited to take our FREE Peak Performance and Salability Assessment to get a better understanding of the attractiveness of your business.

PLEASE SEND YOUR REQUEST TO
INFO@PROFITMAXSOLUTIONS.COM
OR LOG ON TO
WWW.PROFITMAXSOLUTIONS.COM

You've got to seize the opportunity if it is presented to you.

Clive Davis

YOU'RE INVITED...

You're invited to take advantage of our FREE Peak Performance and Salability Assessment to get a better understanding of the attractiveness of your business.

What you will discover from this powerful session:

- The overall financial health of your business
- Key elements that are sabotaging the growth of your business
- How your small business stacks up against the competition
- The areas in your business that are robbing you of additional value

AND...

- How you can turn your business into a highly profitable, revenue-generating machine that can be sold for more money than you thought possible in a way that's easier than you ever imagined!

This 45 minute session was designed to help business owners learn how they can transform their business into an asset that can be worth double or triple its current value providing the most money when they're ready to exit.

**PLEASE SEND YOUR REQUEST TO
INFO@PROFITMAXSOLUTIONS.COM
OR LOG ON TO
WWW.PROFITMAXSOLUTIONS.COM**

ABOUT THE AUTHOR

Justin K. Cauley is a Small Business Profit and Growth Expert that has dedicated 10 years to helping small businesses increase revenue, increase profit, and increase and manage cash flow. Justin is an entrepreneur and business development consultant who enjoys working with business owners looking to create a business that can virtually run on autopilot, allowing the business to be sold successfully when the owner is ready.

Justin has worked with business owners across the United States and in several foreign countries. His expertise has been used by banks, lending institutions, CPAs, attorneys, business buyers/sellers and entrepreneurs dedicated to taking their business to the next level.

Justin actively participates in projects within his community, fraternity, and other organizations both locally and abroad. He received his M.B.A. from The University of Wisconsin and his B.S. from Drexel University.

Justin K. Cauley